CO-CREATE WITH YOUR UNIVERSE

PRINCIPLES OF MANIFESTATION

ROSALINE BOSCO MAHIMAIDOSS

ISBN 979-888530976-9

This book is dedicated to every person that has travelled with me until now, in the journey of Life. You have played a part in transforming my life for the better, by providing invaluable experiences. I thank my parents, husband, children, grandchildren, assistants and my pets in a very special way for all the enriching learning experiences they have given me throughout my life and for their support in varying circumstances of life.

Contents

Foreword

There is nothing physical about this Universe. Everything about our Universe is connected to the mind. A gradual evolution of our Consciousness has led us to a magnificent place, where we realize that everything that we need can be achieved through our mind, and only through our mind. Any physical object or reality of whatever magnitude can be materialized through our mind. There is no exception to this Universal Law.

Quantum Physics has revealed some startling truths about our Universe. Quantum is the Latin word for amount and, in modern understanding, means the smallest possible discrete unit of any physical property, such as energy or matter. Individual units of energy were named as Quanta by Planck.

One of the most startling revelations made by Quantum Physics was through the Double Slit Experiment. The experiment done by Thomas Young in 1801 revealed that Light and Matter can function both as particles and waves at the same time. They assumed the characteristic of a particle when they were observed and functioned like a wave when they were left unobserved.

This left the scientists quite baffled as they were unable to explain the phenomenon of how something could function both as a wave and as a particle at the same time. But this discovery revealed that the laws of Nature cannot be explained by Science and everything in this Universe is made of pure energy, which upon observation, can manifest or change into matter. In short, we can manifest all our dreams just by following some Laws that the Universe has modeled for us.

These Laws are not meant to benefit only the human species but all animate and inanimate things, because everything has Consciousness. There is no matter. Matter is just an illusion created for us living in the Earthly plane to make our lives easier to manage. Time and Space are also such constructs to make our experiences seem real, and for the convenience of Linear and Progressive Time. But Time does not exist in other Dimensions. Millions of Near Death Experiences have proved this.

Waves of probabilities surround us, and it is left to us to manipulate or use them in such a way, that we can change those waves of potentiality into matter, to achieve our dreams and goals.

There are certain rules and conditions for us to follow to change these waves of probability into Reality. These Principles will be expounded in the following chapters.

Preface

YOU ARE A CO-CREATOR WITH THE UNIVERSE

How exciting is this possibility of knowing that you create your own Reality!

Convince the Universe, to conspire with you, in designing the best experiences for you in this lifetime, even beyond your expectations.

Can you convince the Universe to do this?

Yes. Surely you can. You can convince the Universe to bend reality for your sake.

Just imagine manifesting everything that you need with minimum effort.

We are at the threshold of a major shift, that is occurring in the Universe and it is in our hands to make the best use of it, and manifest the best for ourselves and all around us.

How do we use this magic key which we possess, that has been entrusted into our safe keeping?

How has it become possible for this great shift to occur now?

How can we make the best use of this change of Consciousness that is spreading through our Planet like wildfire?

You can find the answers to all the above questions in this book.

These answers are insights obtained through experiences gained by interacting with the Universal Laws of Creation and Co-Creation.

But these laws are not connected with matter, as we have believed so long. These laws are embedded in the LAWS OF CREATION and CO-CREATION of our Universe.

Acknowledgements

I acknowledge the power of the Holy Spirit and the power of the Supreme Consciousness which is the Source of all creation. I acknowledge the work of my grand daughter Michelle Deborah Dixie, who created the cover page.

CO-CREATE WITH YOUR UNIVERSE

PRINCIPLES OF MANIFESTATION

ROSALINE BOSCO MAHIMAIDOSS

CHAPTER ONE

EXPAND YOUR HEART CHAKRA AND MAGNIFY YOUR MAGNETIC FIELD

Love is the most important tool for manifesting your reality!

Any act that is done out of Love expands your Heart Chakra.

When you practice pure love, you may not see immediate results but the reward comes back to you when you are in dire need. It can be a lifesaver in dangerous circumstances.

It is good Karma that you have accumulated, that will come to your aid when you are in an adverse situation. It is a saving that can be used later. You can never be sure when this act of Love that you have performed is going to fructify and bear fruit.

The laws of the Universe are irrevocable. They cannot be changed.

Any act of love, done in a selfless manner is recompensed. When we expand our heart, the immediate result is bliss. Many of us do not have the luxury of seeking solitude to meditate in the mountains.

When we express or do acts of love intentionally, and without seeking anything in return, the immediate aftereffect is joy.

Expanding the Heart Chakra enhances our aura in a positive manner.

The aura or human energy field is a colored emanation which surrounds a human body or any animal or object. In Spiritual parlance, the aura is described as a subtle body. Kirlian photography is able to capture the auras of individuals where the colour of a person's essence is captured. Our Aura has different colours according to the positive or negative feelings that we possess.

Love comes directly from our heart and it can influence the electromagnetic fields that surround us.

It creates waves of probabilities. This in turn creates a lot of opportunities to attract all that we need in Life.

It attracts good relationships.

It attracts positive thinking and joy.

It attracts abundance and enhances our personality.

It attracts opportunities to improve our financial conditions as well.

A simple exercise can help you to expand your Heart Chakra.

Place your hand over your heart for a few second every day. You can repeat this whenever you feel overwhelmed by emotions. This is also a gesture of expressing Love for self.

Self Love does not mean selfishness.

When you love yourself unconditionally you are also able to love others unconditionally.

Make this your mantra

I Am Love. I share this Love with those around me.

Love makes me joyful and enhances my aura.

Through Love I can attract waves of potentialities or probabilities.

When I give Love, I also receive Love.

Society has trained us to think that only material rewards are valuable. But there are other factors like health, peace and happiness which can be attracted through expanding our Heart Consciousness. The Universe loves to stay in touch with those who have an expanded heart.

CHAPTER TWO

STOP COMPLAINING, START MANIFESTING

The idea that we are all energy forms is really exciting, and this leads us to the understanding that we are truly unlimited in nature. At the same time the principles of manifestation need to be followed in order to reap the best results. The most important rule of manifestation is that we should stay aligned or be in harmony with the Universal Laws in order to achieve all that we need.

The most important principle that is needed to start this process is to stop complaining. The Universe is not in favour of anybody who complains and groans and mumbles his or her way through Life. Rather, it is the greatest and the most ardent supporter of anybody, who faces adverse situations and challenges, with grace and loving acceptance.

How many of us can truly say that we do not complain about anything in Life? Some of us complain about our spouses, some about our workplace, our bosses, traffic, children, the climate, and it seems as if our tolerance levels are coming down.

Definitely there is an endless list of situations that we can complain about in our daily lives. Or we can look at these situations as challenges that we can overcome with patience and fortitude. Remember that the Universal Spirit remains as a spectator within us every second of the way, and knows all our inclinations, fears, emotions and prejudices. We cannot fool something that is within us.

The challenges that we face are real, but a slight change in perspective can go a long way. Everyday challenges can be considered as mind games that the Universe plays with us to check our strength.

Here I do not refer to serious situations where a person may have to face a terminal illness or a catastrophe in Life. I refer only to the ordinary incidents in Life which might seem intolerable to us.

The reason why complaining acts as a deterrent against attracting is because, when we complain our frequency is reduced to a very low level. As a result we fail to connect with the plans of the Universe.

On the other hand when we realize that we can change the situation by altering our attitude, we become aligned with the functioning of the Universe. The Universe becomes our best friend in whatever enterprise we desire to undertake, and also ensures that we succeed in our effort.

CHAPTER THREE

FEEL GRATEFUL! ATTRACT AND MANIFEST ALL YOUR DESIRES

I cannot emphasize enough, upon the importance of feeling grateful for all that we have in our lives. Most of us throw away the magnificent plans the Universe has for us, through our ungrateful attitude!

Just contemplate on how parents would feel when children constantly complain and grumble in spite of all that they do for them. There is a breaking point when everything comes to a standstill.

The experiences we have during our lifetimes are based on our previous actions, and they are the result of the cause and effect relationship of all our accumulated actions of our past.

How can it help when we also add the additional burden of being ungrateful? But we can definitely mitigate the pain of adding more to the imbalance, by feeling grateful to the Universe.

Remember that we can reduce the evil effects of our past actions by increasing our vibrations and level of frequency.

How do we communicate with our Universe, The Cosmic forces, The Guardian Angels, The Ascended masters, The Spirit Guides and our own loving Ancestors who have passed before us?

This is not something which is impossible to achieve. It can be done through practising all the steps that I have detailed in the following pages.

The Universal Spirit is the mother/father of all Conscious things around us. There is nothing around us which does not possess Consciousness. Everything around us is throbbing with Consciousness. We are not aware of it because the wavelength in which everything vibrates is not visible to our naked eyes.

Talk to your loving parent, the Spirit which pervades through all Consciousness, in your own language, from your heart and the Universe will respond to you through synchronicities and miracles. This is a small prayer of Gratitude which you can modify according to your choice.

PRAYER OF GRATEFULNESS TO THE UNIVERSAL SPIRIT

Dear Universe

You are the beginning! You have no end!

You are infinite and unlimited in potential and magnitude.

I Am a part of your magnitude and potential.

You are the source of unlimited and unconditional Love.

I Am your child and I am also a source of unlimited and unconditional Love.

I Am grateful for all that you have given to me.

I Am grateful for my parents, brothers and sisters and all my family members.

I Am grateful for the beauty of Nature that surrounds me.

I Am grateful for the beauty of my mind and wisdom that you have endowed me with.

I Am grateful for good Health.

I Am grateful for the house that I live in.

I Am grateful for my career.

I Am grateful for the vehicle I possess.

Every second of my life, I live in gratitude for all that the beauty that you have brought into my life!

Thank you! Thank you! Thank you!

This prayer can be modified according to the list of things you feel grateful for. This, in turn will increase your frequency and vibration level.

CHAPTER FOUR

YOU, AND ONLY YOU ARE THE PROTAGONIST OF YOUR LIFE, BELIEVE IN YOURSELF

This Principle is worth repeating over and over again because it is the foundation of a major part of our suffering in Life. Society has molded us through institutions for thousands of years to make us believe that we are not the main characters of our own lives.

How can this affect us? It affects our interactions with others because we believe that our major role is to change the people around us according to our own way of thinking.

On the contrary, when we start believing that the journey of life is meant for our own personal growth and transformation, and not meant to transform others, except though example, Life become a source of joy.

You can make this your personal narrative and alter the prayer according to your choice

I am the main character of my Life!

I am my own heroine/ hero.

Everybody else plays a supportive role in my Life.

Their role is to help me grow in Self Realization.

In this drama of Life, I am meant to overcome my own challenges with their support.

My role is not to transform them.

They can only change through overcoming the loving challenges posed by the Universe for their growth.

When I try to manipulate or find shortcuts to transform my family members or friends, I become unsuccessful in my attempts, because I cannot defeat the specific challenges planned for them by the Universal Spirit.

The Universe is more knowledgeable than me in transforming everyone in the most perfect way imaginable.

When I try to interfere with the Life Lessons meant for others, through arguments and conflicts, I reduce my frequency and my positive vibrations.

In short I reduce my power to attract more.

I fail to go 'inside' and focus on my own lessons and challenges that the Universe, or my Higher Self have so lovingly designed for me in the most unique way. My constant complaining against others makes me an unhappy soul, and creates an aura of negativity around me.

Everybody else is the hero/heroine of his or her own story.

He or she is perfectly entitled to change his or her Life story at any point of time.

Anybody can initiate a loving communication with the Universe, and can experience the nurture and unconditional Love of the Universal Spirit.

When I learn from my challenges and change myself, I cooperate with the Universe and help it to transform those who live around me.

I invite more and more miracles into my life. I can experience the love of the Universe in a very intimate manner. The following prayer can help us understand that we only need to play a supportive role in other people's lives.

Dear Universe

Help me to look deeply inside myself to change into the beautiful butterfly that I was meant to be. Give me the understanding that when I do not focus on myself but on others, I belittle your unconditional mercy and love for my brothers and sisters. In addition I create an aura of negativity around me.

I have been created to achieve my greatest potential and to be the main actor in my own life.

CHAPTER FIVE

LOVE AND VALUE YOURSELF UNCONDITIONALLY

Though the purpose of Life is to achieve success, it does not mean that we should fall into the abyss of guilt and shame when we face failure. The following can be your personal narrative to value yourself unconditionally.

The journey of Life is to help me realize my greatest potential!

Some of the Life lessons which have been designed by my higher self in collaboration with the Universal Spirit are quite challenging in nature.

I cannot expect to achieve success at the very first attempt and come out with flying colors.

If I fail in my attempts, the Universal Spirit, in its unconditional loving essence, allows me to try until I succeed.

It gives me chances through many lifetimes to transform myself into the brilliant multi faceted diamond that I was supposed to be.

I am not meant to hate myself for my failures. When I hate myself for my failures I also fail to love myself unconditionally. Thus I refuse the Love of the Universal Spirit which has created me, with unconditional acceptance.

I value myself and will try over and over again to overcome my imperfections.

I respect myself unconditionally, and will not allow others to condemn, judge or treat me in an unloving manner.

I realize that the Universe collaborates and cooperates with me in all my efforts to become better and encourages me with rewards and miracles every step of the way.

These rewards may not exactly be the rewards that I imagine for myself in the material realm, but can be the greatest and the best that the Universe, in its absolute intelligence, deems to be the best for me in my circumstances.

I love myself and I will never let down the Universe by believing that I am lesser than what I AM.

When I love myself unconditionally, and become non judgmental about myself, I also stop judging others. I am able to love them in spite of their personal beliefs and experiences in Life.

CHAPTER SIX

FORGIVE YOURSELF! MANIFEST THE BEST

Some religious leaders project the human ideas of conditional Love and a punishing God, even though the Ascended Masters of all Religions preached Unconditional Love and Forgiveness. This is because the human nature of the leaders in these religious sects does not permit them to imagine a God who does not punish mortals for their fallibilities.

As a result of this propaganda many human beings wallow in guilt, shame and self pity and have almost given up on themselves. It is good to realize the following when a person is consumed by guilt and feelings of shame.

I have incarnated on Earth only with the mission of learning my Soul Lessons.

I cannot learn my Lessons without making mistakes.

I cannot evolve unless I face challenging situations in Life.

I may fail or succeed initially but I will never stay stuck in gloom forever.

I will rise up like the Phoenix with the realization that God is not judgmental.

It is my own Higher Self which counsels me during my learning experiences.

I will not allow others to set impediments upon my path of learning.

I will not believe people who have lost their faith in me, and as a result lose faith in myself.

I understand that Life Review happens to enable me to reach the highest level of Consciousness and become one with the Divine Energy.

I understand that it is the unwritten Law of the Universal Consciousness that no one will be left behind in this journey towards Source or God Consciousness.

It is just a matter of time for different people to learn their Soul Lessons. Some may be slow learners but it does not mean that they will never pass their challenges of Life. In view of these conditions I will forgive myself for the times I have failed in my life and rise up to succeed in the future.

I understand that when I forgive myself unconditionally, I am also able to forgive others, without projecting my own vulnerabilities upon them.

When I forgive others as the major Religions and Ascended masters advise me to do, I become one with the Spirit of the Universal Consciousness. This in turn helps me to materialize my heart's desires and makes all my dreams come true.

CHAPTER SEVEN

HEAL YOURSELF, MANIFEST MORE

It is now time for us to understand that we have been conditioned by the views of the material world to such an extent, that we have absolute faith in what it has to offer. This has moved us a long way from the world of Nature that God has created for us in such exquisite detail.

Each one of us has been transformed to a vast degree by our social upbringing, which makes us slaves to hierarchical structures of status, gender, race and other inequalities.

Many of us have been brainwashed by the society to believe that the rich are greater than the poor, the mightier are more powerful than the weak and the male is superior to the female.

These assumptions are made on perfectly transient factors which are subject to change drastically. The rich can become poor and the poor can become rich. The female of the species can exhibit more will power than the male at times.

A person from a different race can overcome adversity and have abundant wisdom, enough to transform the world through Love.

The following can be your personal narrative when you desire to heal yourself.

I am perfect in every way.

Everything that I have experienced in my Life has made me what I am today.

There is nothing in me that I need to feel ashamed about.

All my experiences, whether positive or negative, from my point of view, are for my personal growth and evolution of my Consciousness.

I can heal myself from my past trauma and emerge as a more loving and knowledgeable person.

My traumatic experience need not necessarily drain me, if I realize that I was meant to go through it for my own good.

My trauma need not necessarily make me afraid of the world that I live in.

My trauma need not necessarily make me hate the world that I live in.

My trauma need not necessarily make me septic or anti social.

I am fully capable of healing myself from the incidents that have occurred in my life.

I pray for forgiveness from those who I have hurt because of my own weaknesses.

The purpose of existence is to learn unconditional Love through Forgiveness.

By healing myself, my frequency and vibration are enhanced and I am able to attract Abundance.

This is because the Universal Spirit appreciates my understanding and value for self.

The Universal Spirit acknowledges me as an essential part of itself, and sends me more love, because when I heal myself, I also heal a part of the Universal Consciousness.

I now consciously heal myself completely from all experiences which have troubled me.

CHAPTER EIGHT

FORGIVE THOSE WHO HAVE HURT YOU! ATTRACT ABUNDANCE

Once you have forgiven yourself and healed yourself completely, it is very simple to forgive others. This is because you really hold others accountable for what you consider as sinful, in your own mind.

When you stop projecting this Consciousness upon the nature of others by forgiving yourself for your mistakes, then forgiveness of others becomes relatively simple.

We are reminded of the Lord's Prayer

Forgive us our trespasses,

As we forgive those who sin against us!

The Universal Spirit requires that we forgive others so that we can be forgiven our own mistakes. This is also exactly why Christ said that every woman/man should make peace with her/his brother/sister on Earth before offering worship to God. You can make the following narrative your own, using words which are contextually suitable.

I forgive my brother or sister who, I think has hurt or has done me injustice.

I do this wholeheartedly and with no compulsion from anybody else.

I understand that the wrongful action committed by my brother or sister was his, or her own lesson to learn.

It is not my duty to bear this vengeance in mind.

Nor is it conducive to my own well being to punish the brother or sister who knowingly or unknowingly acted against me.

The Universal Spirit is the best guide and has a plan for correcting errors through its own impeccable system of Retribution and Justice.

The Universal Spirit does not expect me to become self righteous and engage in the act of punishing my brother or sister who has wronged me.

On the other hand I earn the appreciation and admiration of the Holy Spirit, when I forgive those who have wronged me.

This I do in the fullest measure, without an iota of regret or feeling of anger that I have been wronged.

Forgiving those who have wronged us can be truly achieved through practice. It is also a skill which can be learned. Constant repetition of the above narrative will convince you of the importance of forgiving others. Send positive thoughts from your mind, to those who you feel, have wronged you.

When this is done constantly we are freed from the heavy burden of having to forgive others, and the task becomes light and easy.

CHAPTER NINE

LIVE IN THE NOW! MAKE 'MIRACLES' HAPPEN

I can assure you that this is one of the most important tools for manifesting your desires. I also reiterate that unless you practice the previous principles given in this book it is very difficult to stay in the 'now.'

The Universal Spirit has arranged Time in a linear sequence only for convenience, so that it becomes easier for us to travel this earthly journey in a sequential manner.

It helps us to measure our progress on the Timescale. Near Death experiences reveal that Time does not exist in Heaven nor is it linear. Out of body experiences and Spiritual experiences also reveal that the Future as well as the Past can be accessed in the present.

So we live our lives afresh every second. We grow through experiences.

The greatest mistake committed by humans is getting stuck to their pasts and failing to make use of the present.

Just imagine this scene! You are stuck in the traffic and the past comes up in your mind where your boss confronted you for coming late to work.

Just stay in the 'present' without thinking too much, and things will get sorted out automatically. Your boss himself might be stuck in the traffic that day. He/ She might be in a better frame of mind in the present. Who Knows! Your boss might be doing a course on 'How to stay in the present?'

Living in the 'now' has incomparable advantages in family relationships, especially between the spouses. Generally in marital discords, many incidents get magnified as they seem to be a repetition of the past.

Be aware that each incident has occured in a different timeline, and may not have the same context. It might not be an intentional repetition. Assuming that it has been done intentionally might result in a conflict.

When a partner is late from work, it is better to approach the incident in the present context. It is also essential to realize that a person does not change through conflict. Only internal change can help in transformation.

Understand that it is not in your power to change anybody. Only the Universal Spirit can aid a transformation. Though it might take a long time for the person to change, it cannot be stopped. The All knowing Spirit can work these changes miraculously but only in its own infinite wisdom and patience.

Let this be you personal narrative when you face such situations.

This is my experience in the present! It has nothing to do with the past.

I live my life in the moment, and my present is not connected to the past.

Linear Timeline is just a matter of convenience, to help me to grow as a part of the Universal Consciousness.

I will stay focused on my present situation. The Universal Spirit has a unique plan by which it fulfills its role through this incident.

When I stay aligned with the Universal Spirit in the present, I can overcome any problem in Life.

Let me tell you my dear friends that you are now moving along the road of being a miracle worker and a seasoned magician, who can make synchronicity, happen.

CHAPTER TEN

GO WITH THE FLOW!
DO NOT OFFER ANY RESISTANCE TO THE UNIVERSAL SPIRIT

This is one of the most difficult principles to follow but can be achieved through constant practice. It is difficult to practice because we assume that we know the best always. But sometimes we may not be aware of the bigger picture.

The Spirit of the Universe is the source of knowledge and is the source of all creation. It sees the whole picture and not as segments from an individual perspective. Even the simplest of actions carries a 'ripple' effect, which has the potential to influence hundreds of people through a chain reaction.

Imagine a person who feels depressed and unloved, being transformed by a simple smile and in turn feeling loved and valued.

It would cause an impact in her/his family and the society who she or he is in contact with. A single act of Love can transform a person contemplating suicide, and inspire a will to live. These are not fantasies but real life experiences. There is an intricate web connecting our Consciousness to those around us in particular and the world in general.

The media gives us the impression that we are separate from the others and that we should fear everything. It sensationalizes every event for its own gains.

From an individual point of view, we might not have complete understanding about the nature of an incident or why things had to happen the way they did, for greater good.

We try to induce changes in another's behavior thinking that we know the best. But every person has a learning experience through which change occurs. We cannot simplify the path for another person by resisting or through arguing the case.

It does not mean that we should completely ignore unfavorable traits and accept them. When a friend or a family member is reluctant to change even after constant reminders it is best to let God take care of the issue instead of opposing the situation with all our strength.

When we resist something constantly, and it seems that we are banging against a brick wall, it is good to stop fighting it and let the Universe do the rest.

It is very important to Go with the Flow!

Or we might be resisting the flow of the Universe and fighting against it with our own will. We might be fighting against an opponent whom we could never win.

Let this be your personal narrative when you try hard to resist something in your life.

The Universal Spirit does not work for individual good but works for the Collective good.

Trying to resist a situation over and over again will not yield success.

Let us be like water which takes the shape of the vessel that it is poured into.

Going with the flow does not mean that I should not act prudently in an adverse situation.

On the contrary it means acting with presence of mind, for the best of all concerned, without creating conflict or disharmony.

If the situation cannot be changed after trying many times, it is better to allow things to unfold by themselves.

When I go with the flow I cooperate and become a Co-Creator in the Universal plan of Action.

It becomes easier to manifest 'abundance' and 'synchronicities' when I work together with the Almighty Spirit.

CHAPTER ELEVEN

DETACH THE EGO SELF, GIVE CREDIT TO THE UNIVERSE, BECOME A MAGNET FOR MANIFESTING

This principle may take time to practice but it is very beneficial in the long run. Our society has become obsessed with competition and success. Children are forced to compete for the best results, and achievers receive much acclaim. But a majority are not high achievers. They are above average or just average performers.

Since the expectations of the society is very high, we have become accustomed to compete in all areas, from the time we are born till the end of our lives. So it may be difficult to detach the Ego self from our achievements. If our achievements lead us to help others who are vulnerable or weak, it can give us permanent satisfaction. Realizing that we are gifted with a particular talent, and that this gift is not what we earned through merit, but something that we are blessed with, can make us more grounded.

Being more talented, rich, beautiful or powerful is also a challenge posed to us by the Universal Spirit.

These gifts are not meant to make us proud or feel superior to another, but to enable us to use this gift to benefit others as much as possible.

God never intended us to have an inflated Ego because we are more blessed than others. The intention behind every gift is to ascertain that we do not become greedy, selfish and power conscious.

This can become your personal narrative.

I have been blessed with this gift- mention your specific gift or skill.

This is not something which I earned but something that I was born with.

This talent need not necessarily make me feel superior to others.

I am not in competition with another.

I am happy for the unique gift that another person is blessed with.

I will spend my talent to benefit as many as possible and not only to profit myself.

The Universal Spirit does not intend me to use my gift only to benefit myself.

The purpose of my gift is also to help others to progress.

When I do this, I align myself with the Universe and it becomes possible for me to manifest my desires easily.

CHAPTER TWELVE

OUR EARTH IS A CONSCIOUS BEING! BECOME ONE WITH NATURE TO MANIFEST

We have always taken for granted that we are superior to other living beings on Earth. We have also assumed that all Natural resources are meant primarily for human beings, to be used as we like. This has led to an over exploitation of natural resources as we find it difficult to curtail our needs.

As a result we are currently combating huge natural disasters such as floods, earthquakes, tsunamis and forest fires.

How do we move forward at this critical juncture?

Everything in the cosmos has Consciousness!

How do I know this?

Quantum Physics has proved the effect of the 'observer' on the 'observed' through the Double Slit Experiment. The Double Slit experiment proves that we can change results in a measurable way, through our mental faculties or observation.

This is also called 'constructive interference' in Physics.

Every atom in the Universe is vibrating at its own speed, in its own frequency.

An atom in any part of the world influences another, simultaneously without time interference. This is called Quantum Entanglement.

This realization is the first step in moving forward. Everything in the Universe is also evolving the same way as the human species. So when we cause extensive damage to a part of the Universe it is like pricking our own eye.

This can be corrected if each of us accepts the following.

I am not the sole proprietor of this Universe.

I share this Universe along with other creatures.

The rest of Creation also has a rightful place in this Universe.

I live in a Conscious Universe.

Whatever I do affects my planet and in turn affects the whole Universe.

I am also a part of this Consciousness and I am not separate from it.

I cannot continue to pollute my Planet.

If I continue to pollute my planet, I am ruthlessly destroying the future of my planet as well as the prospects of the future generations.

I will stop focusing on being selfish, and make wise choices and decisions which will not harm my planet.

I will be responsible in taking care of my planet and also educate those who are unaware of the dangerous situation that we are in.

I will play a role in increasing Consciousness among my brothers and sisters.

I will respect every single organism in the Universe.

By doing the above I show my love for the Universe that I live in. I will attract all the good things that the Universe has to offer, like a magnet.

Recent researches prove that everything including plants, water and other living and non living things are Conscious. For example plants respond to love, and grow better in loving circumstances. Even water responds favorably to loving words and becomes disoriented and muddled when rude words are spoken over it.

CHAPTER THIRTEEN

GO 'WITHIN' AND KNOW YOURSELF TO REAP THE BEST REWARDS

The desire to change others happens because of our belief that we know better than our Creator. But change is a process that can only be initiated from within and not from the outside.

Our Ego tempts us to believe that we can change those around us to fit our personal likes and dislikes.

Why doesn't this work?

It is because in this situation, we separate ourselves from the Universal Spirit. We believe in personal skill and do not act in Cooperation and Co-Creation with God.

The 'secret' is not to go 'outside' and try to effect change, but change from 'within' ourselves.

This requires us to be in a state of constant awareness and in a self introspective state. It does not mean self condemnation for our thoughts and emotions, but being in the 'observer' state and realizing that there is an 'observer' who is present in all situations.

Ancient sages and rishis practiced this in caves and mountains. But we are obliged to practice this in the midst of the challenges that we face in everyday life. The ability to practice this self introspective state, in the midst of interacting with different personalities is equally commendable.

You can make this your personal narrative.

God has the infinite power and wisdom to create transformation in the Universe.

My role is to go 'within' and be the observer to make effective changes within myself.

I need not go to great lengths to judge or change anybody.

My duty is to play a supportive, loving and non judgmental role in all my interactions.

Being judgmental creates conflict.

When I play a non judgmental, supportive role towards others, the Universe enables me to Co-Create with it.

CHAPTER FOURTEEN

THE SECRET KEY TO MANIFESTATION! REALIZE THAT YOU ARE AN ETERNAL BEING

When does manifestation become really quick?

When the Principles of Life mentioned in the previous chapters are understood, manifestation becomes very quick.

There may be certain characteristics which might operate as blocks and prevent us from reaching out to the Universal Spirit. When we understand the blocks that are preventing us, and change them the blocks are cleared.

After awareness is created, the block is gradually removed even if it is not removed immediately.

A major block that prevents us from communicating with the Universe is the fear of the unknown. We live in constant dread about the uncertainty of the future and our failures in the past, never living in the moment.

Millions of near Death Experiences prove that we are much more than mere bodies and that we are not limited by Space and Time even after we leave our bodies. We are Eternal beings and are powerful. We enter this world to have different experiences which we cannot have in the spiritual realms.

But once we awaken to our true nature, here on Earth, we can get rid of our pettiness.

When we awaken to this new reality, we move into a new Dimension of living, which is equal to Heaven on Earth. All our notions of being weak and vulnerable are shattered.

We realize that we have been 'hoodwinked' from the time we were born. We have been raised to compete, in the belief that we should overtake others, and be the best.

When we realize that every single one of us is a part of the Collective and that our experience on Earth is a very small percentage of our experiences as eternal beings, our competitive nature is smashed into smithereens.

The understanding, that we are capable of manifesting much more than material possessions and that we are spiritual beings is a very exciting prospect to ponder over.

We need not wait for an enterprising entrepreneur to take us to Space at an exorbitant monetary value. We already know that Space is ours, after we eradicate our limiting beliefs.

You can make this your personal narrative to realize that you are an eternal Being

I AM not vulnerable, weak or thrive on mere competition.

I AM a powerful eternal being.

I AM the heir to the Source of unconditional Love and pure Consciousness.

When I rise, I lift others along with me.

When I lower my frequency, I bring the others down along with me.

I have risen over my limiting beliefs.

I AM ETERNAL, FLAWLESS AND PURE. MY JOURNEY ON EARTH IS AN AID TO THIS AWAKENING OF WHO I TRULY AM.

CHAPTER FIFTEEN

PRACTICE RANDOM ACTS OF KINDNESS!
RAISE YOUR FREQUENCY FOR EASY MANIFESTATION

We believe that the opposite of Love is Hate, as it is defined in dictionaries.

But the opposite of Love is Fear!

When we go deep inside we realize that it is fear which keeps us slaves to all our limiting beliefs.

The first tool to raise frequency is Love. Just as charity begins at home, Love too begins with the family. We start by sharing Love with relatives and friends. The next step would be to extend this love to those who are struggling to keep themselves afloat on the ocean of Life. The Love that we share can elevate us to a higher frequency, if it is unconditional. If you are able to love a Brother or sister who has harmed you, your frequency is elevated to a much greater level than you can imagine.

Practicing Random Acts of Kindness is a very important way of sharing our Love. It means helping even a stranger you meet, when it is possible for you to do so.

Love can be extended through random acts of kindness towards people whom the Universal Spirit draws towards us. When we do this we are elevated to the next grade at once.

The Universal Spirit becomes an indulgent Father who has no choice but to help us realize our aspirations when we raise our frequency through kindness. Since we act selflessly in such situations, it becomes possible for us to manifest and uplift those around us.

This can be your narrative to increase your frequency.

I AM not meant to live in fear of the future.

I AM a child of pure Love.

I AM able to love others, beyond my limited family circle of relatives and friends.

I AM able to practice random Acts of Kindness along my journey in Life.

I love myself! I love others!

CHAPTER SIXTEEN

MAKE MEDITATION JOYFUL!
PRAYER, MUSIC AND NATURE INCREASE YOUR FREQUENCY

Prayers are very powerful!

They have a frequency which can elevate you to the highest level possible. Prayers that have been constantly uttered or chanted by millions of people all over the world, acquire a very elevated level of frequency.

They help to combat negative energy and protect us from great dangers.

Some Near Death experiences, especially in the cases reported by children reveal that the frequency of Prayer rises like a rainbow in multi colored hues to the sky.

Music can also elevate us to a great degree.

According to Madam Blavatsky, "The sound has an attractive property, it draws out disease, which streams out to meet the musical wave, and the two, blending together, disappear in Space."

Just like the power of Prayers, Music also elevates us to a very high level of frequency. 417 Hertz, 528 Hertz and 432 Hertz are some powerful healing frequencies in music. 432 Hertz is referred to as 'The God Frequency.'

Listening to soothing music is as healing as a meditative practice, and when this is done regularly this also acquires great power of its own. This can be considered as joyful meditation because when we become absorbed in the lyrics we forget our problems.

Being one with Nature is one of the greatest ways in which our frequency can be elevated. Nature is also the greatest healer in the world. Many people, who have had an awakening experience, develop an invigorating relationship with Nature. They develop great love towards Nature and God's creations. This can also be accompanied by synchronicities and a deeper Faith in Spirituality.

Staying away from arguments and conflicts also increases our frequency.

On the contrary having a great sense of humor and unbridled joy can increase our frequency.

When we vibrate at a higher frequency, we are at the best of our creative capacity. Meditation need not be serious. The more that we are able to passionately involve in a spiritual practice, the more effective it becomes. Being consistent is the key. Indulging in Creative Arts can also become meditation when it comes from the Soul

You can make this your personal narrative

I will not indulge in actions that will reduce my frequency.

I will engage in positive activities like Prayer, Music, Meditation, and having a sense of humor, which will increase my frequency.

When I reduce my frequency, it becomes impossible for me to attract abundance in my Life. This is because I move away from the Love and Light of God.

CHAPTER SEVENTEEN

YOUR INTENTIONS ARE VERY IMPORTANT! BE AUTHENTIC

The Universe loves authenticity. Universal Spirit cannot be fooled by pretensions.

Our thoughts have a very important role in attracting results in our lives. Being your own self and acting with genuine intentions bring forth incredible results.

All of us cannot have the same personalities. Differences between human beings make every person unique.

God has determined that it should be that way, for interaction between souls. This would help one human being to learn from another.

From the spiritual point of view, a soul has no choice but to learn from another through many lifetimes and through many relationships. Every person has a good quality that another can learn. Authenticity or the nature of being true to oneself is evident in the lives of Godly people.

An example of one such incident in the life of Jesus Christ was when he multiplied bread loaves and fish for those who came to listen to his sermon. When our intentions are focused more on the larger good, it becomes easier to attract abundance. Saints and seers have made miracles happen, when they were meant to benefit a large number of people.

Being authentic attracts positive occurrences in our lives. A genuine intention is always reciprocated by the Universe. When any action is performed with an ulterior motive it may not bring the expected results

You can make this your personal narrative.

I AM authentic in all that I say and do.

I AM always true to my intentions and the principles that I represent.

I do not pretend to be somebody that I AM not meant to be.

That will never endear me to the Universal Spirit.

Rather, my efforts to stay authentic in all that I say and do will endear me to the Universal Spirit and help me attract all my dreams.

CHAPTER EIGHTEEN

SEPARATION IS AN ILLUSION! BELIEVE IN THE COLLECTIVE CONSCIOUSNESS TO CO- CREATE

We enter this earth with a veil of forgetfulness. We have forgotten our true home.

Our true home is a place where there are no separations like religion, status, ethnicity, gender and caste that we presently have on Earth.

These are manmade differences to exploit others.

Being in constant awareness, that we are only playing the character that has been chosen by us here, and that other actors are also acting their own roles is very important.

This is very important because when we feel separate from the others, we move away from God. Our accomplishments might make us believe that we are superior to others.

Such thoughts have to be overcome. Belief should be reinstated in a single Consciousness, which can be called Christ Consciousness or Brahma Consciousness or the Buddha Consciousness according to various religious ideologies. It should be realized that every living organism is a part of this Collective Consciousness, and contributes towards its growth.

This can be your personal narrative.

I AM a drop in the ocean of the Collective Consciousness.

I AM not separate from the others.

When I treat another as different from me in status, religion, caste or gender I discriminate against her/him.

Every single experience that I have had in my life has made an impression in the Collective Consciousness.

I AM constantly aware that I should make a positive impact with my every action and raise the Collective Consciousness.

We are all meant to evolve as a whole human Consciousness towards the sublime.

When I AM aware of this, I can Co-Create my reality with my Universe.

CHAPTER NINETEEN

BE AN 'OBSERVER' OF YOUR OWN LIFE

Do not become obsessed with the 'role' that you play in Life.

When you become obsessed, you end up feeling frustrated and defeated.

Give hundred percent to Life, but stay detached from the results of your actions.

When we become too attached to actors and their actions, we become 'reactive.'

Playing the role of the 'observer' keeps us calm and composed.

In addition it prevents conflicts.

We begin to realize that each creates his/her reality by being himself / herself, learns through experiences, and changes to attract a better reality.

We cannot take the Law of the Universe into our hands to punish anybody.

Nor can we play the role of the Judge to condemn anybody.

The Universal Spirit is the best Judge! It has infinite patience, mercy and wisdom.

Surrender to the Holy Spirit of the Universe and remain a 'passive' observer of your own Life.

You can make this your narrative

I AM not the 'role' I play.

I AM an observer of all that is.

Playing an observer's role liberates me from suffering.

It frees me from the bondage of taking responsibility for other people's actions.

My frequency is raised high enough to become one with the frequency of the Universe.

Conclusion

A nutritious meal contains proteins, carbohydrates, vitamins and minerals in the right amounts.

An imbalance can either cause undernourishment or obesity. Similarly, currently there is an imbalance in the society, where a few exploit the masses. It is not the way in we were supposed to live.

This is causing major environmental problems and natural disasters. The solution lies in achieving balance. Only a balanced approach can save our Earth.

The younger generation is very much aware of how we are ruthlessly polluting our planet.

Earth is also a Conscious being.

When we rise up together as a unified entity, our Earth would become the Heaven

that we have been longing for.

Heaven is not a physical place but a dimension in Consciousness.

This book is an invitation to create Heaven on Earth.

THE END

You can reach me at rosalinebosco@yahoo.com

My YouTube Channel https://studio.youtube.com/channel/UC0CXPfabNPsWZm2cNSX4LLA

Printed by Libri Plureos GmbH in Hamburg,
Germany